STEP·BY·STEP

SPANISH

Cooking

KÖNEMANN

BASIC SPANISH PANTRY

Most of the ingredients for Spanish cooking can be found in your local supermarket. Those few unusual ingredients, such as Chorizo sausage, which are only available at selected delicatessens, can be successfully replaced with substitutes (in the case of Chorizo, with spicy salami).

Ali-oli: An egg-based mayonnaise, heavily flavoured with garlic.

Almonds: There are many uses for almonds in Spanish cooking in both savoury and sweet dishes. Almond meal is very finely ground blanched almonds. It is used in soups, sauces and cakes in the same way as flour.

Capsicums: Green and red capsicums are used extensively throughout Spanish cookery. To peel capsicum, place it under a hot grill, or holding it with long-handled tongs, turn it over a gas flame until the skin blackens. Set aside until cool, covered with a clean dampened tea-towel. The black skin will flake off easily and the capsicum will have a delicious smoky flavour.

Chick peas: Also known as Spanish beans, garbanzo or ceci peas. They have a nutty flavour and a crisp texture. Chick peas require long soaking (about 8 hours) before cooking. Canned chick peas, usually labelled as garbanzo, may be substituted without loss of taste or texture.

Chorizo: Spiced coarsely textured red sausage eaten extensively throughout Spain. Any spicy salami may be used in its place.

Garlic: Fresh garlic is used extensively and is best crushed on a wooden board with the point of the blade

of a large knife. A small amount of salt added to the garlic before crushing will produce a paste.

Herbs: Spanish cookery uses a variety of herbs all of which are readily available to us. Best used fresh but if unavailable, dried may be substituted (reduce the quantity). The most commonly used herbs are rosemary, thyme, sage, basil, mint and parsley.

Olive Oil: There is no substitute for the taste of olive oil and Spain produces some of the best. Experiment with different brands to find the one that best suits your taste buds.

Onions: Spanish or red onions are readily available at most greengrocers. They

are milder and sweeter than brown onions and are delicious when eaten raw in salads. When unavailable, substitute white or brown onions, depending on the recipe.

Paella: The most well known of all Spanish dishes. The ingredients vary from region to region, depending on the local produce but it always contains rice flavoured with garlic, saffron (or turmeric) and olive oil.

Paellera: The name of the large, flat, two-handled pan used solely for the purpose of cooking the most famous rice dish, Paella. Any large, heavy-based frying pan or shallow pan may be used.

Paprika: A spice made from a variety of sweet pepper grown extensively through Europe. It is a deep rich red colour and has a mild aromatic aroma with a strong earthy flavour. Sweet paprika is most commonly used but a hotter variety is also available.

Pine Nuts: The kernel from the cone of certain types of pine tree that grow around the Mediterranean coasts. Available from most supermarkets or health food stores.

Rice: Plain boiled rice is rarely served in Spain – rice is usually coloured with saffron or turmeric, or flavoured with fried onions, or cooked with other ingredients as in Paella. Long-grain rice gives the best results.

Saffron: Available ground or in stigmas. It is an expensive spice and may be difficult to obtain. If unavailable, a small amount of either turmeric or ground sweet paprika may be used in its place.

Sherry: Spain produces some of the world's best sherry. from dry through to sweet. Both are used in many sweet and savoury foods.

Tomatoes: Almost every savoury recipe contains tomatoes for both colour and flavour. Use ripe red full-bodied tomatoes. If unavailable, canned tomatoes are an excellent substitute.

Vinegar: Wine vinegar both red and white are always used in Spanish cookery. If unavailable, white and malt vinegars may be substituted.

Using a sharp knife slit open the octopus head and remove the gut.

Pick up the body and use the index finger to push the beak up and remove.

STARTERS & SOUPS

These starters and soups, like most Spanish food, are rich and robust and use lots of garlic. Serve in small quantities.

Grilled Baby Octopus

Tender and delicious.

Preparation time:
15 minutes +
2 hours marinating
Cooking time:
6 minutes
Serves 4-6

---

18 baby octopus
2 teaspoons finely grated lemon rind
1/4 cup lemon juice
1/4 cup olive oil

2 cloves garlic, crushed
1/4 cup chopped fresh parsley
1 tablespoon ground sweet paprika

---

1 To clean the octopus, use a small sharp knife and remove the gut by either cutting off the head entirely or by slitting open the head and removing the gut.

2 Pick up the body and use the index finger to push beak up. Remove. Clean octopus thoroughly. Remove eyes. Cut sac into 2 or 3 pieces and set aside.

3 Combine lemon rind, juice, olive oil, garlic, parsley and paprika in a large bowl. Add prepared octopus, cover with plastic wrap and marinate 1-2 hours.
4 Lightly oil a grill, arrange octopus evenly over surface and cook under medium-high heat 3 minutes each side while spooning over marinade. Serve hot or cold.
Note: For extra flavour marinate the octopus pieces 2-3 days, turning them every day.

Combine lemon rind, juice, oil, garlic, parsley and paprika in a bowl.

Cook under medium high grill 3 minutes each side while spooning over marinade.

Wrinkled Potatoes with Mojo Sauce

Preparation time:
20 minutes
Cooking time:
25 minutes
Serves 4-6

---

18 baby new
  potatoes
1 tablespoon olive oil
2 teaspoons salt

SAUCE
2 cloves garlic
1 teaspoon cumin
  seeds

1 teaspoon ground
  sweet paprika
1/3 cup olive oil
2 tablespoons white
  wine vinegar
1 tablespoon hot
  water

---

1 Preheat oven to moderately hot 210°C. Place potatoes in single layer in a baking dish. Pour over oil, shake pan to distribute oil evenly. Sprinkle salt evenly over potatoes.

2 Bake 20-25 minutes or until potatoes are golden brown and slightly wrinkled. Shake pan twice during cooking time.

3 To make Sauce: Place garlic, cumin seeds and paprika into bowl of food processor. Blend for 1 minute. With motor constantly operating, add oil slowly in a thin stream, blending until all oil is added and sauce has thickened slightly. Add vinegar and hot water and blend 1 minute longer.

4 Serve potatoes hot accompanied by a spoonfull of Sauce.

Note: Mojo sauce originated in the Canary Islands and is served throughout Spain in Tapas bars. Another version of this sauce uses finely chopped coriander leaves in place of paprika. This is served with fried fish. Wrinkled potatoes are also good served with garlic mayonnaise (Ali-oli) , especially with fish.

Pour oil over potatoes then sprinkle salt over them evenly.

Bake until potatoes are golden brown and slightly wrinkled.

Blend together for 1 minute, the garlic,
cumin seeds and paprika.

With motor operating, add oil slowly in a
thin stream then add vinegar.

Spanish Pizza

The ideal snack.

Preparation time:
30 minutes
Cooking time:
45 minutes
Serves 4-6

BASE
7 g dried yeast
1 teaspoon caster sugar
2¼ cups plain flour
1 cup warm water

TOPPING
10 spinach leaves, shredded
1 tablespoon olive oil

2 cloves garlic, crushed
2 medium onions, chopped
1 x 440 g can tomatoes, drained and crushed
¼ teaspoon ground pepper
12 pitted black olives, chopped

---

1 Preheat oven to moderately hot 210°C. Brush a 30 x 25 x 2 cm Swiss roll tin with melted butter or oil.

2 To make Base: Combine yeast, sugar and flour in a large bowl. Gradually add warm water; blend until smooth. Knead dough on a lightly floured surface until smooth and elastic. Place it into a lightly oiled basin, cover with a thick towel and leave to rise in a warm position for 15 minutes or until the dough has almost doubled in bulk.

3 To make Topping: Place spinach in large pan, cover and cook on low heat for 10 minutes. Drain spinach and cool. Using hands, squeeze out excess moisture, set aside.

4 Heat oil in medium pan; add garlic and onions. Cook over low heat 5-6 minutes. Add tomatoes and pepper, simmer gently for 5 minutes.

5 Punch dough down, remove from bowl and knead on lightly floured board for 2-3 minutes. Roll dough out to fit prepared tin. Spread with spinach, top with tomato mixture and sprinkle over olives.

6 Bake 25-30 minutes. Cut into small squares or fingers. Serve hot or cold.

Note: In Spain the base of the pizza is made from leftover bread dough from the local baker. The base can also be made from scone dough or shortcrust pastry.

HINT
Yeast dough may be made the day before required. Place into large container or bowl, cover and refrigerate. Next day, punch down, knead lightly and roll out. When making a yeast dough it is always advisable to warm the flour in the oven first. This helps the dough to rise more quickly.

Gradually add warm water to flour, yeast and sugar in bowl.

Knead dough on a lightly floured surface until smooth and elastic.

Add tomatoes and pepper to cooked onion and garlic in pan.

Spread dough with spinach and top with tomato mixture then olives.

Chilled Tomato Soup

Preparation time:
15 minutes +
1-2 hours
refrigeration
Serves 4-6

---

3 slices white bread, crusts removed

8 large ripe tomatoes, peeled, seeded and chopped

1 cucumber, peeled, seeded and chopped

1 small onion, chopped

1 small green capsicum, chopped

1/3 cup chopped fresh mint

2 cloves garlic, crushed

2 tablespoons olive oil

2 tablespoons red wine vinegar

2 tablespoons tomato paste

1-2 cups iced water

GARNISH

1 medium red capsicum, cut into thin strips

1 medium onion, thinly sliced

1 small cucumber, peeled, seeded and chopped

2 hard-boiled eggs, chopped

1/2 cup sliced green olives

---

1 Combine all ingredients except iced water in a large bowl. Cover with plastic wrap and stand for 20 minutes.
2 Divide mixture into thirds. Place one third into food processor bowl. Using the pulse action, press button for 30 seconds or until smooth. Pour mixture into large bowl; repeat with remaining two batches. Thin mixture to desired consistency using iced water. Cover with plastic wrap and refrigerate for at least an hour.
3 Serve soup in large or individual bowls with ice cubes. Garnishes are placed in small bowls and passed around for guests to add to soup as desired.

Note: This soup is known throughout the world by its Spanish name, *Gaspacho.* It is the most well-known of Spanish soups. It is always served cold and is a very refreshing way to start a summer meal. Tomatoes must be ripe so as to achieve the best flavour. Remember to remove seeds. Canned tomatoes may be substituted if fresh are not available.

HINT
To remove tomato seeds cut tomato in half after peeling and gently squeeze. Any remaining seeds may be removed with a teaspoon. To seed cucumbers, cut them in half lengthways and remove seeds with a teaspoon.

Combine all soup ingredients except iced water and stand for 20 minutes.

Place one third of the mixture into the food processor and blend until smooth.

Use the iced water to thin the soup to the desired consistency.

Chop garnishes and place in small bowls for guests to add to soup as desired.

Garlic Soup

Adjust chilli to suit.

Preparation time:
15 minutes
Cooking time:
30 minutes
Serves 4-6

¼ cup olive oil	*1 teaspoon ground*
6 cloves garlic,	*sweet paprika*
crushed	*½ teaspoon chilli*
1½ cups fresh white	*powder*
breadcrumbs	*1 L water*
3 medium ripe	*2 eggs, lightly beaten*
tomatoes, peeled	*¼ cup chopped fresh*
and chopped	*parsley*

1 Heat oil in large pan; add garlic. Cook over gentle heat 1-2 minutes until soft but not brown. Add breadcrumbs and cook over medium heat 3 minutes or until they turn a light golden brown.
2 Add tomatoes, paprika, chilli powder and water. Bring to the boil; simmer, covered, 30 minutes.
3 Add eggs in a thin stream to simmering soup. Cook over low heat 2 minutes longer.
4 Pour into serving bowl, sprinkle over parsley and serve.
Note: Serve hot and heavily seasoned.

Heat crushed garlic in oil over gentle heat until soft but not brown.

Add breadcrumbs and cook over medium heat 3 minutes or until golden.

Add tomatoes, paprika, chilli powder and water and simmer for 30 minutes.

Add beaten eggs in a thin stream to simmering soup; cook 2 minutes.

White Fish Soup

A lemon-flavoured soup served over a slice of toast.

Preparation time:
25 minutes +
1-2 hours
marinating
Cooking time:
15 minutes
Serves 4-6

---

1 kg white fish fillets	*3 bay leaves*
3 small red onions, chopped	*¼ cup olive oil*
3 cloves garlic, crushed	*2 tablespoons white wine vinegar*
¼ cup finely chopped fresh parsley	*1 L fish stock*
2 teaspoons finely grated lemon rind	*1 cup dry white wine*
¼ cup fresh lemon thyme leaves	*¼ teaspoon ground pepper*
	4-6 thick slices of white bread

1 Remove all skin and bones from fish fillets and cut into 2.5 cm pieces. Place fish into a large bowl.
2 Combine onions, garlic, parsley, lemon rind, lemon thyme, bay leaves, olive oil and vinegar. Pour mixture over prepared fish, cover with plastic wrap and leave to marinate in the refrigerator for 1-2 hours.
3 Place fish mixture into a large pan, add stock, wine and pepper. Bring slowly to simmering point and simmer covered for 15 minutes or until fish is just tender.
4 Just before serving, toast bread on both sides until golden brown. Place into individual bowls and pour hot soup over. Serve immediately.
Note: We used perch in this recipe but any white fish or combination of fish may be used. Traditional Spanish bread is oval in shape and has a very crisp crust. French bread may be substituted.

Cut white fish fillets into 2.5 cm squares and place in a large bowl.

Combine onions, garlic, parsley, lemon rind, lemon thyme, bay, oil and vinegar.

Spoon the mixture over the fish, cover and leave to marinate.

Place mixture into large pan and add stock, wine and pepper.

Cook potatoes and onion over medium high heat until golden brown.

Once potato is cooked through remove and drain on absorbent paper.

EGGS & RICE

Eggs and rice are staples in Spain where Paella is often known simply as 'rice' and the Potato and Onion Omelette is called 'Tortilla'.

Potato and Onion Omelette

Preparation time:
15 minutes
Cooking time:
20 minutes
Serves 4-6

2 tablespoons olive oil	4 eggs
2 large potatoes, cut into 1.5 cm cubes	1/4 teaspoon ground sweet paprika
2 medium onions, chopped	1 tablespoon olive oil, extra

1 Heat oil in medium heavy-based pan; add potatoes and onions. Cook over a medium-high heat until golden brown and well coated with oil. Reduce heat, cover the pan and cook for 5-6 minutes, stirring occasionally, until potato is cooked.
2 Remove potato and onion from pan. Drain on absorbent paper. Beat eggs and paprika in a medium bowl until frothy; gently stir in potato-onion mixture.

3 Heat extra oil in clean pan. Add egg mixture and cook covered over medium heat 15-20 minutes or until mixture is firm. Place under hot grill until golden brown.
4 Serve hot or cold cut into wedges with a simple salad.
Note: The success of this omelette relies on slow even heat, which is why you need a heavy-based pan. A non-stick pan may also be used. It prevents the omelette from sticking and also reduces the amount of oil needed by half.

Beat eggs and paprika in a medium bowl until the mixture is frothy.

Gently stir the potato-onion mixture into the egg mixture.

Flaming Eggs

Hot and spicy.

Preparation time:
25 minutes
Cooking time:
25 minutes
Serves 4-6

2 tablespoons olive oil	2 tablespoons tomato
1 small onion,	paste
chopped	6 eggs
1 small red capsicum,	12 thin slices spicy
chopped	salami
1 teaspoon finely	2 tablespoons chopped
chopped red chilli	fresh parsley
1 x 440 g can	
tomatoes, crushed	

1 Preheat oven to moderately slow 160°C. Heat oil in medium pan, add onion and cook over medium heat until soft and lightly golden. Add capsicum and chilli, cook 2-3 minutes longer. Add tomatoes and tomato paste and cook uncovered over low heat for 10 minutes, stirring occasionally.

2 Transfer tomato mixture into shallow ovenproof dish. Using the bowl of a soup spoon, press six hollows into the mixture to hold the eggs. One-by-one carefully break each egg into these prepared hollows.

3 Top mixture with salami. Bake for 20-30 minutes or until whites are set and yolks are still soft.

4 Sprinkle with parsley and serve immediately.

Note: In Spain the salami that would traditionally be used for this dish is a coarsely textured red sausage called Chorizo. Any of your favourite salamis can be substituted.

This is an excellent dish to serve for brunch or a light lunch accompanied by a crisp green salad and crusty bread.

Add capsicum and chilli to cooked onion in pan and cook a further 2-3 minutes.

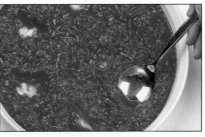

Using a soup spoon, press hollows into the tomato mixture to hold each egg.

Carefully break an egg into each prepared hollow.

Cover each egg with two slices of salami and bake for 20-30 minutes.

19

Egg and Zucchini Scramble

Preparation time:
15 minutes
Cooking time:
15 minutes
Serves 4-6

---

1 tablespoon olive oil	*1 small green*
1 large onion,	*capsicum, chopped*
chopped	*2 large ripe tomatoes,*
4 rashers bacon,	*peeled and chopped*
chopped	*6 eggs*
3 small zucchini,	*¼ teaspoon ground*
sliced	*pepper*

---

1 Heat oil in large pan; add onion and bacon. Cook over medium heat until the onion is golden brown and the bacon crisp.
2 Add zucchini and capsicum, cook for 3 minutes. Add tomatoes and cook over low heat for about 4-5 minutes.
3 Place eggs and pepper in medium mixing bowl and beat until well combined. Pour eggs over zucchini mixture and cook until eggs are set, stirring occasionally. Serve immediately with hot buttered toast.
Note: Add a finely chopped fresh red chilli if desired.

Cook onion and bacon in pan until the onion is golden and the bacon crisp.

Add sliced zucchini and chopped capsicum and cook for 3 minutes.

Add chopped peeled tomatoes and cook for 4-5 minutes more.

Pour beaten eggs over vegetable mixture and cook until eggs are set.

Paella

A meal in a pan.

Preparation time:
25 minutes
Cooking time:
20 minutes
Serves 4-6

---

1 tablespoon olive oil	*2 cloves garlic,*
4 boned chicken	*crushed*
thighs, each cut into	*1 medium onion,*
4 pieces	*sliced, top to base*
1 large red capsicum,	*1/2 teaspoon ground*
chopped	*turmeric*
1 tablespoon chopped	*4 cups chicken stock*
parsley	*1 cup frozen peas*
425 g marinara mix	*125 g salami,*
2 cups long-grain rice	*thinly sliced*
1 tablespoon olive oil,	*1 lemon, cut into 6*
extra	*wedges*

---

1 Heat oil in large heavy-based pan; add chicken pieces. Cook over medium high heat 2-3 minutes or until golden brown, turning once. Remove from pan; drain on absorbent paper. Add capsicum, parsley and marinara mix to pan and stir for 1 minute over medium-high heat; remove mixture and set aside.

2 Soak rice in cold water 10 minutes, drain, rinse under cold running water; drain again.

3 Heat extra oil in pan, add garlic and onion, cook on medium heat 1 minute or until golden. Add rice, stir well, making sure rice grains are well coated with oil. Stir in turmeric and stock and cover pan with tight-fitting lid.

4 Bring stock slowly to the boil; stir once. Reduce heat, simmer covered 8-10 minutes. Place chicken on top of rice, cover and cook over low heat for a further 10 minutes.

5 Add capsicum and marinara mix, peas and salami. Cover and cook on low heat for 8-10 minutes or until almost all the liquid has been absorbed.

6 Remove from heat, stand, covered 5 minutes or until all liquid is absorbed and rice is just tender. Separate rice grains with a fork just before serving on a large platter garnished with lemon wedges.

Note: Paella is the best known rice dish from Spain. It takes its name from the shallow round pan or 'Paellera' that it is cooked in. Any shallow pan will make a suitable substitute. There are many variations to the basic Paella recipe – a mixture of prawns, mussels and scallops may be substituted for the marinara mix in this recipe.

Cook chicken pieces in oil for 2-3 minutes or until golden brown.

Add rice to cooked onion and garlic in pan, stirring well to coat with oil.

Stir in turmeric and stock, cover and bring slowly to the boil.

Add red capsicum, marinara mix, peas and salami and cook 8-10 minutes.

Rice Valencia Style

Preparation time:
10 minutes
Cooking time:
15 minutes
Serves 4-6

1¼ cups long-grain rice	2 teaspoons finely grated orange rind
1 tablespoon olive oil	½ cup orange juice
15 g butter	½ cup sweet sherry
1 medium onion, chopped	1½ cups chicken stock

1 Soak rice in cold water 10 minutes, drain, rinse with cold water; drain again.

2 Heat oil and butter in a medium pan over low heat. Add onion and cook until golden brown and soft; add rice, reduce heat to low. Stir rice 2 minutes or until lightly golden.

3 Add orange rind, juice, sherry and stock. Cover pan with tight-fitting lid. Bring to the boil; stir once. Reduce heat, simmer, covered 8-10 minutes or until almost all liquid is absorbed. Remove from heat, stand, covered 5 minutes or until all liquid is absorbed. Separate rice grains with a fork and serve.

While rice is soaking in cold water, peel and chop onion.

Heat oil and butter, add onion and cook until golden brown and soft.

Add the rice, reduce the heat and stir for 2 minutes or until light golden.

Add orange rind, orange juice, sherry and stock, cover and bring to the boil.

VEGETABLES & SALADS

Most of these vegetable dishes can be served as a course on their own, some of them as a meal on their own, with fresh crusty bread.

Tomato and Capsicum Stew

Preparation time:
15 minutes
Cooking time:
15 minutes
Serves 4-6

2 tablespoons olive oil
1 large red onion, chopped
2 large red capsicums, chopped
1 large green capsicum, chopped
4 large ripe tomatoes, peeled and chopped
2 teaspoons brown sugar

1 Heat oil in medium pan; add onion. Cook over low heat until onion is soft.

2 Add red and green capsicums and cook over medium heat for 5 minutes, stirring.

3 Stir in tomatoes and brown sugar. Reduce heat, cover and cook for 6-8 minutes until vegetables are tender.

Chop red and green capsicums into squares and chop onion lengthways.

To peel tomatoes, make a small cross at top and place in boiling water.

Add capsicums to softened, but not browned, onions in pan.

Add tomatoes and brown sugar, reduce heat and cook covered 6-8 minutes.

Mixed Grilled Vegetables with Garlic Mayonnaise

Preparation time:
  30 minutes
Cooking time:
  15 minutes
Serves 4-6

GARLIC
MAYONNAISE
2 egg yolks
4 cloves garlic,
  crushed
1 cup olive oil
pinch pepper
2 tablespoons lemon
  juice

VEGETABLES
4 small eggplants

4 medium red
  capsicums
4 medium firm
  tomatoes
4 small onions
1/3 cup olive oil
1/3 cup chopped fresh
  parsley
1 clove garlic, crushed
1/4 teaspoon ground
  pepper

1 To make Garlic Mayonnaise: Place egg yolks and garlic into a medium mixing bowl. Whisk together for 1 minute. Add oil, about a teaspoon at a time, whisking constantly until mixture is thick and creamy. Increase addition of oil as mayonnaise thickens. Stir in pepper and lemon juice. Set aside.

2 Place whole unpeeled vegetables onto lightly oiled grill. Cook under hot grill 6-8 minutes, turning once, until they are black all over; remove, cover with clean wet tea-towel and allow to cool slightly. Peel blackened skin from vegetables and cut into 2 cm cubes. Arrange them in a serving dish.

4 Combine olive oil, parsley, garlic and pepper in a small bowl and pour over vegetables. Serve hot or tepid as a course on its own accompanied by Garlic Mayonnaise and Spanish bread.

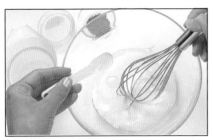

To make mayonnaise add oil a teaspoon at a time until mixture is thick.

Place whole unpeeled vegetables onto a lightly oiled grill.

Peel blackened skin from vegetables and cut into 2 cm cubes.

Combine olive oil, parsley, garlic and pepper in a small bowl.

Orange and Spinach Salad

Preparation time:
15 minutes
Serves 4-6

4 medium oranges	*⅓ cup olive oil*
10-12 spinach leaves	*¼ cup red wine*
1 medium red onion,	*vinegar*
sliced	*¼ cup toasted pine*
½ cup pitted black	*nuts*
olives	

1 Place each orange on a board, cut a 2 cm slice off each end to where the pulp starts. Peel, removing all white membrane.

Separate segments by carefully cutting between membrane and flesh with a small sharp knife. Do this over a bowl so you don't lose the juice.

2 Break spinach into bite-sized pieces, place into a large bowl. Add sliced onion, orange and black olives.

3 Place olive oil and vinegar in a small bowl. Whisk until well combined.

4 Pour dressing over salad and toss to mix well. Place into serving bowl, sprinkle with toasted pine nuts and serve the salad immediately.

Cut a 2 cm slice off the end of each orange, then peel thickly.

Separate segments by cutting between membrane and flesh over a bowl.

Add onion, orange segments and olives to torn spinach leaves in bowl.

To make dressing, whisk together olive oil and vinegar in a small bowl.

Asparagus and Artichoke Salad

Preparation time:
20 minutes
Cooking Time:
10 minutes
Serves 4

---

*1 bunch fresh
asparagus
130 g green beans
150 g button
mushrooms
5 canned or
marinated
artichoke hearts
30 g butter
1/2 teaspoon ground
sweet paprika*

*2 cloves garlic, sliced
thinly
2 tablespoons olive oil
2 tablespoons lemon
juice
1/4 teaspoon black
pepper
2 tablespoons finely
chopped mint*

---

1 Cut asparagus spears into 5 cm lengths. Trim the tops off beans, leaving tails on. Cut mushrooms in half and artichoke hearts into quarters.

2 Half fill a medium saucepan with water, bring to the boil. Place asparagus and beans into the boiling water for 1-2 minutes or until they turn bright green. Remove from heat. Plunge into a bowl of iced water and leave until chilled; drain.

3 Heat butter in a small pan. Add paprika and garlic, cook for 1 minute. Add mushrooms, cook 2-3 minutes; remove from heat.

4 Combine oil, lemon juice, pepper and mint in a small bowl. Mix well. Place asparagus, beans, mushrooms and artichokes in a medium bowl. Pour over oil mixture and toss well. Transfer salad to serving bowl.

Note: Plunging green vegetables into cold water after cooking helps to retain their colour and flavour. This salad can be made with capsicum, broad beans, carrots, peas or zucchini.

Cut up asparagus, beans, mushrooms and artichoke hearts.

Boil asparagus and beans and then plunge into iced water.

Add mushrooms to the butter, paprika and garlic in pan.

Mix together in a small bowl, oil, lemon juice, pepper and mint.

Carrot with Salami and Raisins

Preparation time:
15 minutes
Cooking Time:
15 minutes
Serves 4-6

---

2 tablespoons olive oil
10 thin slices spicy salami, cut into strips
15 g butter
6 medium carrots, finely chopped

4 spring onions, sliced
1/2 teaspoon cumin seeds
1/2 teaspoon ground cinnamon
1/2 cup raisins
1/4 cup pine nuts

---

1 Heat oil in large pan; add salami. Cook over medium heat 2 minutes or until just crisp. Remove and drain on absorbent paper. Remove any excess oil from pan.

2 Heat butter in pan; add salami, carrots, spring onions, cumin seeds and cinnamon. Cover and cook over low heat 4 minutes or until the carrots are just tender.

3 Add raisins, cook 3 minutes longer, add pine nuts and shake pan to combine.

4 Serve alone or as an accompaniment to grilled or baked meat or chicken.

Cut salami into strips and cook in olive oil until crisp.

Remove from pan and drain well on absorbent paper.

Add salami, carrots, spring onions, cumin seeds and cinnamon to pan.

Add raisins, cook 3 minutes, then add pine nuts.

Cut chicken into serving-sized pieces using poultry shears or a cleaver.

Add tomatoes, plum sauce, wine and stock to cooked vegetables in pan.

POULTRY, MEAT & FISH

Because of its long coastline, Spain has a tradition of fish dishes. Meat and poultry are most often served in stews and casseroles.

Chicken and Chick Peas in Spicy Tomato Sauce

Preparation time:
25 minutes +
overnight soaking
Cooking time:
1 hour
Serves 4-6

---

3 tablespoons olive oil
1 x 1.5 kg chicken,
cut into serving-
sized pieces
1 small onion,
chopped
2 small red
capsicums, cut into
large squares

1 x 440 g can
tomatoes, crushed
1/2 cup plum sauce
1/2 cup white wine
3/4 cup chicken stock
1 cup chick peas,
soaked overnight
250 g salami, cut
into 1.5 cm squares

---

1 Heat oil in large pan. Cook chicken over medium–high heat 3-4 minutes or until golden brown, turning once. Remove from pan; drain on absorbent paper.

2 Add onion and capsicum to pan, cook over medium heat until onion is soft and golden. Add tomatoes, plum sauce, wine and chicken stock. Simmer uncovered for about 10 minutes.

3 Add chicken and chick peas to pan, cover and simmer 1 hour or until chicken is cooked and chick peas are tender.

4 Preheat oven to 200°C. Transfer mixture to shallow ovenproof dish, top with salami and bake 5-7 minutes or until salami is crisp.

Add browned chicken and soaked chick peas to pan and simmer 1 hour.

Transfer to large ovenproof dish and top with salami; bake 5-7 minutes.

Chicken Spanish Style

Preparation time:
  30 minutes
Cooking time:
  25 minutes
Serves 4-6

6 chicken breast fillets	1 tablespoon plain flour
6 thin slices leg ham	1½ cups chicken stock
toothpicks, to secure fillets	1 cup apple cider
60 g butter	¼ teaspoon ground pepper
1 small onion, chopped	¼ teaspoon ground nutmeg
1 small carrot, finely chopped	¼ cup toasted pine nuts, optional

1 Preheat oven to moderate 180°C. Using a sharp knife, make a deep incision into the thickest section of each breast. Insert a slice of ham and secure with toothpicks. Cover chicken with plastic wrap and refrigerate until required.

2 Heat butter in pan; add onion and carrot. Cook 4 minutes over low heat until onion and carrot are soft. Add flour and stir over low heat until lightly golden. Add combined stock and apple cider gradually to pan, stirring until mixture is smooth. Add pepper and nutmeg. Stir constantly over medium heat 3 minutes or until sauce boils and thickens; boil further 1 minute. Remove from heat.

3 Place chicken in single layer in shallow ovenproof dish. Pour sauce over, cover and bake 20-25 minutes.

4 Remove toothpicks from chicken and serve with a spoonful of sauce. Top with pine nuts.

Note: The apple cider may be alcoholic or non-alcoholic.

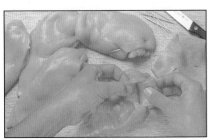

Insert ham into incision in chicken fillet and secure with toothpick.

Heat butter in pan, add onion and carrot and cook for 4 minutes.

Mix together stock and apple cider and add it gradually, stirring until smooth.

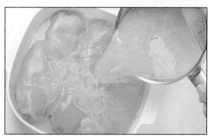

Place chicken in ovenproof dish and pour sauce over; bake 20-25 minutes.

Lamb and Herb Casserole

Preparation time:
  25 minutes
Cooking time:
  45 minutes
Serves 4-6

---

2 tablespoons olive oil
1 small onion,
  chopped
3 cloves garlic,
  crushed
1.5 kg leg of lamb,
  boned and tied
1 teaspoon chilli
  powder

1 tablespoon ground
  sweet paprika
2 medium red
  capsicums, chopped
1 cup dry white wine
2 cups chicken stock
1/4 cup fresh
  rosemary sprigs
1/4 cup chopped fresh
  mint

---

1 Preheat oven to moderate 180°C. Heat oil in large pan; add onion and garlic. Cook over medium heat for 3-4 minutes. Add lamb and cook, turning, until well browned on all sides. Remove lamb and place into deep ovenproof dish.

2 Add chilli powder, paprika and capsicum to pan, stir to combine and cook 5 minutes over medium heat.

3 Add combined wine and chicken stock to pan, stir to combine, bring slowly to the boil, reduce heat and simmer uncovered for 10 minutes. Add rosemary and mint and transfer mixture to jug. Pour sauce over lamb.

4 Cover and bake 45 minutes or until lamb is tender.

Note: This casserole contains no flour which results in a thin but well-flavoured sauce. Traditonally it is eaten from small ceramic bowls, to hold the thin liquid. However if a thicker sauce is preferred, coat lamb with plain flour before browning or thicken the liquid with cornflour which has been blended into a paste.

Add boned and tied lamb to cooked onions and garlic in pan; brown.

Add chilli powder, paprika and capsicum to onion mixture and cook 5 minutes.

Pour in combined wine and chicken stock and simmer 10 minutes.

Add rosemary and mint to sauce and pour over lamb; bake for 45 minutes.

Veal with Almond Sauce

Preparation time:
15 minutes
Cooking time:
15 minutes
Serves 4-6

1/2 cup plain flour	*1/4 teaspoon ground*
1/2 teaspoon ground	*cinnamon*
pepper	*1 1/2 cups chicken*
6 thin slices veal	*stock*
steak	*1/4 cup sweet sherry*
30 g butter	*1/2 cup thickened*
2 tablespoons olive oil	*cream*
1/2 cup fresh white	*100 g whole almonds,*
breadcrumbs	*toasted, optional*
1 1/4 cups (150 g)	
almond meal	

---

1 Combine flour and pepper in a medium bowl. Toss veal lightly in seasoned flour; shake off any excess.
2 Heat butter and oil in a large pan; add veal. Cook over medium-high heat 3 minutes on each side, turning once. Remove from pan; drain on absorbent paper.
3 Add breadcrumbs to pan and stir over medium heat until golden brown. Stir in almond meal and cinnamon. Add chicken stock and sweet sherry gradually to pan, stirring until mixture is smooth. Stir continuously over medium heat 2 minutes or until sauce boils and thickens, stir in cream; boil further 1 minute; remove from heat.
3 Arrange veal on serving plate, spoon over sauce, top with toasted almonds.
Note: Do not substitute dry breadcrumbs for fresh – it will ruin the taste and texture of sauce. The sherry may be replaced with the same amount of Madiera if a stronger flavour is desired.

Toss veal lightly in seasoned flour and shake off excess.

Cook veal over medium-high heat 3 minutes on each side.

Stir almond meal and cinnamon into browned breadcrumbs.

Stir sauce until it boils and thickens then add cream.

43

Meatballs in Sherry Sauce

Preparation time:
35 minutes
Cooking time:
20 minutes
Serves 4-6

---

500 g minced pork and veal
1/2 cup fresh white breadcrumbs
1/4 cup chopped fresh parsley
2 cloves garlic, crushed
2 teaspoons ground sweet paprika
2 tablespoons olive oil
30 g butter
1 medium onion, finely chopped

1 teaspoon ground sweet paprika, extra
1 tablespoon plain flour
1/2 cup dry or sweet sherry
1 cup chicken stock
10 small new potatoes
1/4 cup chopped fresh parsley, extra

---

1 Combine mince, breadcrumbs, parsley, garlic and paprika in a medium bowl. Mix well. Using wet hands, roll the mixture into meatballs the size of walnuts.

2 Heat oil and butter in medium pan; add meatballs. Cook over medium high heat 3-4 minutes until well browned. Remove from pan; drain on absorbent paper.

3 Add onion, paprika and flour to pan and cook stirring for 2 minutes. Add sherry and stock gradually to pan, stirring until mixture is smooth. Stir constantly over medium heat 2 minutes or until sauce boils and thickens.

4 Return meatballs to pan with potatoes, cover and cook over low heat for 20 minutes. Serve sprinkled with chopped parsley.

Note: Large potatoes may also be used as long as they are cut into the same size as the meatballs.

Mix together minced meat, breadcrumbs, parsley, garlic and paprika.

Using wet hands shape mixture into walnut-sized balls.

Add onion, paprika and flour to the pan and cook stirring for 2 minutes.

Return meatballs to pan with same-sized potatoes and cook for 20 minutes.

Pork with Fennel

A distinctive dish.

Preparation time:
35 minutes
Cooking time:
1½ hours
Serves 6

---

1 teaspoon olive oil	*2 tablespoons chopped*
3 rashers bacon,	*fresh chives*
finely chopped	*1 egg, lightly beaten*
1.4 kg pork loin, rind	*30 g butter*
removed	*1 tablespoon olive oil,*
1 cup fresh white	*extra*
breadcrumbs	*½ cup sweet sherry*
1 cup finely chopped	*½ cup orange juice*
fresh fennel	*2 tablespoons red*
1 tablespoon chopped	*wine vinegar*
capers	*1 teaspoon finely*
	grated orange rind

---

1 Preheat oven to 180°C. Heat oil in a medium pan and add the bacon. Cook over medium-high heat for 2 minutes or until crisp. Remove from the pan and drain on absorbent paper.

2 Trim the pork loin of excess fat. Cut through lengthways to open out but do not cut right through. Open out and flatten slightly with the palm of your hand.

3 Combine the breadcrumbs, bacon, fennel, capers and chives in a medium bowl; add egg and stir to combine.

4 Press the stuffing over the opened loin. Roll and tie securely with string.

5 Heat butter and oil in frypan. Cook loin over medium heat 3-4 minutes until evenly browned. Remove from the pan and place into a large baking dish.

6 Scrape sediment from frypan. Add combined sherry, orange juice, red wine vinegar and orange rind. Simmer uncovered for 2 minutes. Pour over pork. Bake for 1½ hours or until cooked through.

7 Remove string from pork loin, slice and place onto heated serving platter, spoon pan juices over and serve immediately.

Note: Serve with steamed vegetables.

HINT

Fennel is a vegetable with a strong aniseed flavour which blends wonderfully with pork. If unavailable use celery hearts.

Fresh breadcrumbs are made by removing the crust from day old bread and placing into a food processor bowl. Using the pulse action, press button for 30 seconds or until bread has crumbled to desired texture. Alternatively, rub the bread over a coarse grater or fine cake cooler.

Cut through the loin lengthways, but do not cut right through; flatten slightly.

Combine breadcrumbs, bacon, fennel, capers and chives; add beaten egg.

Press the stuffing over the opened loin; roll and tie securely with string.

Add sherry, orange juice, vinegar and orange rind to pan; simmer 2 minutes.

Spanish-style Beef Pot Roast

Preparation time:
25 minutes
Cooking time:
1½ hours
Serves 4-6

---

1 x 1.5 kg fillet of beef
⅓ cup blanched almonds, finely chopped
⅔ cup green olives, pitted and finely chopped

1 teaspoon ground cinnamon
1 tablespoon olive oil
1 cup red wine
1 cup beef stock
2 tablespoons tomato paste

---

1 Trim beef of excess fat. Using a sharp knife, make 5 deep cuts in the centre section of the fillet. Combine almonds, olives and cinnamon in a medium bowl.

2 Place almond mixture into pockets of meat, pushing in firmly with a spoon. Tie meat securely with string.

3 Heat oil in large pan; add meat. Cook over medium-high heat 3-4 minutes or until evenly browned. Add combined wine, stock and tomato paste, bring slowly to the boil and simmer covered for about 1½ hours or until beef is tender.

3 Remove meat from pan and set aside covered with foil to keep warm while you reduce the sauce. Bring liquid to the boil and boil uncovered for 10 minutes or until sauce is thick.

4 Serve beef thickly sliced with sauce.

Note: Other cuts of beef or veal may be substituted in this recipe if preferred.

HINT
To blanch almonds, place whole shelled almonds in a bowl and pour over boiling water. Leave for 5 minutes then drain. The skin will slip off easily.

Mix together chopped almonds, green olives and cinnamon in a bowl.

Spoon almond mixture into pockets of meat, pushing in firmly.

Cook tied meat over medium heat 3-4 minutes or until browned all over.

Pour over combined red wine, beef stock and tomato paste.

Seafood with Noodles

Preparation time:
35 minutes
Cooking time:
20 minutes
Serves 4-6

---

500 g green king
prawns
2 boneless fish fillets
(about 250 g)
4 small squid hoods
2 tablespoons olive oil
3 cloves garlic,
crushed
1 teaspoon ground
sweet paprika
1 teaspoon chopped
red chilli

3 small ripe
tomatoes, peeled
and chopped
2 tablespoons tomato
paste
1 cup fish stock
1 cup red wine
1 teaspoon brown
sugar
500 g pasta

---

1 Shell and devein prawns, leaving tails intact. Cut fish into 3 cm pieces. Set aside. Using a sharp knife, cut squid into thin rings. Set aside.

2 Heat olive oil in wok or pan; add garlic, paprika and chilli. Cook on medium-high heat 2 minutes. Add prawns, fish and squid and toss over high heat 3-4 minutes. Remove and set aside.

3 Add tomatoes, tomato paste, fish stock, red wine and brown sugar to pan. Bring slowly to the boil, reduce heat and simmer uncovered for 10 minutes. Return seafood to pan and mix well.

4 Cook pasta in large quantity boiling water until just tender. Drain well. Combine seafood mixture with the pasta and serve immediately.

Note: Any pasta may be used for this recipe such as ribbon pasta, shells, macaroni or penne. This is a spicy dish. Reduce or increase the amount of chilli according to your taste.

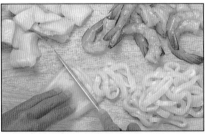

Shell and devein prawns, cut fish into 3 cm pieces, cut squid into thin rings.

Cook seafood over high heat 3-4 minutes; remove and set aside.

Add tomatoes, tomato paste, fish stock, red wine and brown sugar.

Cook pasta in a large pan of boiling water until just tender.

51

Sardines with Tomato Sauce

Preparation time:
30 minutes
Cooking time:
15 minutes
Serves 4-6

TOMATO SAUCE
1 tablespoon olive oil
2 cloves garlic, crushed
1 x 440 g can tomatoes, crushed
1/4 cup white wine
2 tablespoons tomato paste
1/4 cup chopped fresh basil

500 g small fresh sardines
1/2 cup plain flour
1/2 teaspoon ground pepper
1/3 cup olive oil
parsley sprigs, for garnish

---

1 To make Tomato Sauce: Heat olive oil in medium pan; add garlic. Cook over low heat for 2 minutes. Add tomatoes, white wine, tomato paste and basil. Simmer uncovered for about 10 minutes.

2 Cut heads from sardines and discard. Clean body, rinse under cold, running water and pat dry with absorbent paper.

3 Combine flour and pepper in a medium bowl. Toss sardines lightly in seasoned flour. Shake off excess. Heat olive oil in medium pan; add sardines. Cook over medium heat 2 minutes each side until tender. Remove from pan; drain on absorbent paper.

4 Place sardines onto large serving plate, top with Tomato Sauce. Garnish with parsley sprigs and serve immediately.

Note: Green prawns and fresh scallops may be substituted for sardines. Cook in exactly the same way (after having peeled the prawns).

Tomato sauce may be made 1-2 days ahead. Store in refrigerator.

Add tomatoes, wine, tomato paste and basil to cooked garlic in pan.

Cut heads from sardines and clean body; rinse and pat dry with absorbent paper.

Toss sardines lightly in seasoned flour and shake off excess.

Cook in olive oil over medium heat 2 minutes each side or until tender.

Pan Fried Fish with Spicy Vinegar Sauce

Preparation time:
20 minutes
Cooking time:
15 minutes
Serves 4-6

SPICY VINEGAR SAUCE	
1 cup white wine vinegar	*1/2 cup plain flour*
1/4 cup fresh thyme leaves	*1/2 teaspoon ground pepper*
1 spring onion, chopped	*6 (about 600 g) small white fish fillets*
1 teaspoon caster sugar	*3 eggs*
1 teaspoon ground sweet paprika	*1 clove garlic, crushed*
	1 teaspoon ground sweet paprika, extra
	1/2 cup olive oil

1 To make Spicy Vinegar Sauce: Combine vinegar, thyme, onion, sugar and paprika in small pan. Simmer uncovered for about 10 minutes.

2 Combine flour and pepper in a medium bowl. Toss fish lightly in seasoned flour; shake off any excess. In a medium bowl, lightly beat eggs with garlic and paprika until frothy. Dip each fillet into egg mixture and hold up to drain off any excess.

3 Heat oil in a medium pan; add fish. Cook on medium-high heat 3-4 minutes each side until golden brown and cooked through. Remove from pan; drain on absorbent paper.

3 Serve fish immediately accompanied by Spicy Vinegar Sauce.

Note: The egg coating on the fish results in a fine, slightly crisp coating. Fish should be served as soon after cooking as possible, otherwise coating will become soggy. Serve sauce with fish not over it.

To make sauce, combine vinegar, thyme, onion, sugar and paprika in pan.

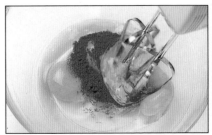

Lightly beat eggs with garlic and paprika until frothy.

Dip flour-coated fillets into egg mixture and drain off excess.

Cook fish 3-4 minutes each side; remove from pan and drain on absorbent paper.

Combine wine, port, orange juice, honey, cinnamon stick and orange rind.

Using a sharp knife, make a slit in each fig from stalk to base.

DESSERTS & CAKES

Spanish desserts and cakes are rich and sweet. The Spanish love custards and sweets made with nuts (especially almonds), dried fruits and honey.

Figs filled with Walnuts and Honey

Preparation time:
30 minutes
Cooking time:
45 minutes
Serves 4-6

---

2 cups red wine
2 cups port
1 cup orange juice
3/4 cup honey
1 cinnamon stick
1 x 5 cm piece of
   orange rind
500 g dried figs

1 1/2 cups walnut
   pieces

SPICED YOGHURT
1 cup plain yoghurt
1 tablespoon brown
   sugar
1 teaspoon ground
   cinnamon

---

1 Combine red wine, port, orange juice, honey, cinnamon stick and orange rind in large stainless steel pan. Bring slowly to the boil, then simmer uncovered for about 10 minutes.
2 Make a slit in each fig from stalk to base and place 3-4 walnut pieces inside. Carefully place figs into simmering red wine mixture. Cover and cook over low heat for 45 minutes.
3 To make Spiced Yoghurt: Combine yoghurt, brown sugar and cinnamon in a small bowl. Cover with plastic and refrigerate for at least 30 minutes before using, to allow flavours to develop.
4 Serve figs warm or chilled accompanied by Spiced Yoghurt.
Note: Yoghurt can be kept refrigerated for 2-3 days.

Open out the slit and place 3-4 walnut pieces inside each fig.

To make Spiced Yoghurt, combine yoghurt, brown sugar and cinnamon.

Orange and Caramel Custard

Serve with cream and strawberries.

Preparation time:
30 minutes +
8 hours
refrigeration
Cooking time:
45 minutes
Serves 4-6

CARAMEL	1 cup cream
1/2 cup water	1 teaspoon finely
1 cup caster sugar	grated orange rind
	3 eggs
CUSTARD	3 egg yolks
1 cup milk	1/3 cup caster sugar

1 Preheat oven to moderately slow 160°C. Brush a deep 20 cm round tin or ovenproof dish with melted butter.

2 To make Caramel: Combine water and sugar in small pan. Stir constantly over low heat until mixture boils and sugar has dissolved. Reduce heat, simmer uncovered without stirring 3-4 minutes or until mixture is dark golden brown. Pour Caramel evenly over base of prepared dish.

3 Heat milk, cream and rind in small pan until almost boiling. Remove from heat; cool and strain. Beat eggs, egg yolks and sugar in a large mixing bowl with electric beaters until thick and pale. Add milk gradually to egg mixture, beating all the time.

4 Pour egg mixture through fine strainer into prepared dish. Stand dish in a deep baking dish. Pour in enough hot water to come halfway up the sides. Bake 45 minutes or until set. Remove dish from the hot water bath immediately.

5 Cool to room temperature and refrigerate for at least 8 hours. Turn out onto serving plate and cut into wedges.

Pour caramel evenly over the greased base of the dish.

Pour the egg mixture through a fine strainer onto the caramel in the dish.

Pour in enough hot water to come halfway up the sides of dish.

Once custard is set remove immediately from water bath and cool.

Almond Lemon Flan

Preparation time:
25 minutes
Cooking time:
40 minutes
Serves 4-6

---

125 g butter, chopped
1 cup caster sugar
4 eggs, lightly beaten
1/3 cup lemon juice
1/2 cup self-raising
  flour
1/2 cup plain flour
2 cups almond meal

LEMON SYRUP
1 lemon
1/2 cup water
1/2 cup caster sugar
whipped cream, to
  serve

---

1 Preheat oven to moderate 180°C. Brush a deep, round 23 cm cake tin with melted butter or oil. Line base and side with paper; grease paper well.
2 Beat butter and sugar in small mixing bowl with electric beaters until the mixture is light and creamy. Add eggs gradually, beating thoroughly after each addition. Add lemon juice, mix thoroughly.
3 Using a metal spoon, fold in sifted self-raising and plain flour and almond meal. Stir until the mixture is almost smooth. Be careful not to overmix.
4 Spoon mixture evenly into prepared tin; smooth surface. Bake 35-40 minutes or until skewer comes out clean when inserted into centre of cake. Stand cake in tin 5 minutes before turning onto wire rack to cool.
5 To make Lemon Syrup: Peel lemon rind into long thin strips and cut into shreds. Combine water and sugar in small pan. Stir constantly over low heat until mixture boils and sugar has dissolved. Reduce heat, add lemon shreds and simmer uncoverd without stirring for 3-4 minutes until a thick syrup has formed.
6 Cut flan into wedges and serve with a spoonful of Lemon Syrup and whipped cream.
Note: To cut lemon rind into shreds, peel rind from lemon using potato peeler or small sharp knife, taking care not to include the white part or 'pith' which will impart a bitter flavour. Using a sharp knife, cut the rind into pieces the thickness and length of a match. If desired, the lemon shreds may be strained from the syrup before serving. For a more tangy syrup, replace part or all of water with lemon juice. The flan and syrup can be made in advance.

Add eggs gradually to butter mixture, beating thoroughly after each addition.

Using a metal spoon, fold in sifted flours and almond meal.

Spoon mixture into prepared tin and smooth the surface.

Peel lemon rind into long thin strips and cut into shreds.

Mocha Torta

Rich and delicious.

Preparation time:
1 hour
Cooking time:
20 minutes
Serves 4-6

---

3 eggs, lightly beaten
2/3 cup caster sugar
2 tablespoons hot
water
1 cup self-raising
flour, sifted

MOCHA CREAM
1/2 cup caster sugar,
1/3 cup water
4 egg yolks

1 tablespoon instant
coffee powder
250 g unsalted butter,
chopped
1/4 cup milk
2 tablespoons rum
100 g toasted flaked
almonds

SAUCE
1 x 425 g can plums

---

1 Preheat oven to 180°C. Brush a 30 x 25 x 2 cm Swiss roll tin with melted butter. Line with paper.

2 Beat eggs 3 minutes or until thick. Add sugar gradually, beating until pale. Fold in water and flour quickly.

3 Spread mixture into tin. Bake 15-20 minutes; leave in tin 3 minutes. Turn onto paper sprinkled with icing sugar.

4 To make Mocha Cream: Combine sugar and water in pan. Heat stirring until mixture boils. Simmer uncovered without stirring 2 minutes; cool. Beat egg yolks and coffee powder until thick. Pour cooled syrup in a thin stream onto egg mixture, beating constantly. Beat butter until light and creamy. Pour egg mixture over butter, beating 4 minutes. Chill 15 minutes.

5 Line base and sides of 26 x 8 x 6 cm bar tin with foil. Trim edges of sponge. Cut into three lengthways. Combine milk and rum. Divide Mocha Cream into three.

6 To assemble Torta: Place one layer of sponge upside down into tin. Pour half rum mixture over surface. Using a spatula spread with one portion of Mocha Cream. Repeat process with second layer. Top with last sponge and press down firmly with hand. Cover with plastic and refrigerate 1 hour or overnight. Turn cake onto serving plate, leave to stand 10 minutes, cover top and sides with remaining Mocha Cream and toasted almonds.

7 To prepare Sauce: Remove stones from plums. Place in food processor bowl. Process until smooth. Serve Mocha Torta sliced with a spoonful of Plum Sauce.

Fold water and flour quickly and lightly into egg mixture with a metal spoon.

Pour cooled syrup in a thin stream onto egg yolk and coffee mixture.

Sprinkle half the milk and rum mixture evenly over cake.

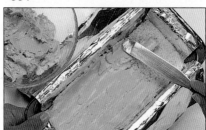

Spread one portion of the Mocha Cream evenly over the surface of the cake.

INDEX

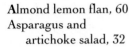